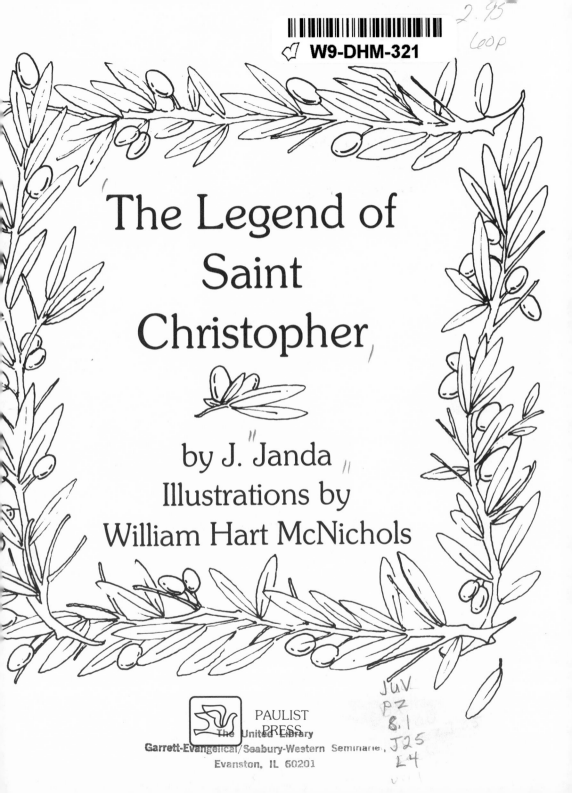

The Legend of Saint Christopher

by J. Janda

Illustrations by

William Hart McNichols

PAULIST PRESS

Text designed by Ellen Whitney

Library of Congress Cataloging-in-Publication Data

Janda, J. (James), 1936-
    The legend of St. Christopher.

    1. Christopher, Saint—Legends—Juvenile literature.
[1. Christopher, Saint.   2. Saints]   I. McNichols,
William Hart, ill.   II. Title.
BX4700.C57J36   1987   398.2′2   [92]   87-15749
ISBN 0-8091-6569-4 (pbk.)

Published by Paulist Press
997 Macarthur Boulevard
Mahwah, NJ 07430

Printed and bound in the
United States of America

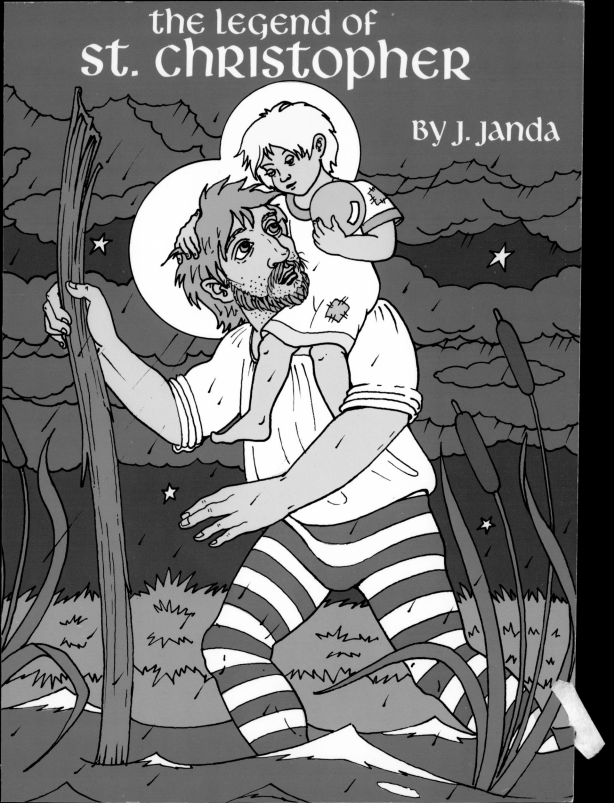

For William Hart McNichols
who encouraged me
to retell the Legend of Saint Christopher

Foreword

You can see many pictures of saints holding the Christ Child, but Christopher is the only one who carries the Christ Child on his shoulder: and the Christ Child always carries a little ball, and Christopher is always walking with a stout pole.

Before I begin, I must tell you that Saint Christopher's name was Reprobus. He took the name Christopher after he met the Christ Child. You will find out all about that later on—so let's begin.

1

Everybody was afraid of Reprobus. Do you know why? Everybody was afraid of Reprobus because he was a giant. Yes, he was over twelve feet tall, almost twice the height of most people.

And if his height didn't scare people, his face did. It's not that Reprobus was ugly, it's just that he was so big: his nose, his eyes, and his ears were bigger than most people's—and that is what scared everybody. People ran when they saw Reprobus coming.

But that did not hurt his feelings; he just smiled and let them go their own way. He was actually a very gentle soul.

Reprobus had one wish—and this wish was the only thing he ever wanted. Do you know what his wish was? His wish was to find and serve only the most powerful man in the world.

And his wish came true, or so he thought at the time, because he met the King of Canaan, and everybody said, "The King of Canaan is the most powerful man in the world."

Well, Reprobus was very happy doing things for the King of Canaan, because he believed that this King was the most powerful man in the world.

The King would say, "Reprobus, help me onto my horse," and Reprobus would pick up the King and put him on his horse.

Or the King would say, "Reprobus, an army is about to attack." All Reprobus had to do was stand in front of the city gate: when the enemy came and saw Reprobus, they ran the other way.

Well, one night while the King was having a big banquet, Reprobus noticed that the King got scared when one of his jesters sang a song about the Devil. The King was so scared that he made the Sign of the Cross whenever the word "Devil" was mentioned. Reprobus finally asked the King why he was so frightened.

And the King replied, "Reprobus, the Devil is nobody to fool with. I have seen people act like the Devil, and believe me, that scares me."

"You mean," said Reprobus, "that the Devil is more powerful than you?"

"In a sense, yes," said the King. "As I said before, he is nobody to play with."

"Well," said Reprobus, "if the Devil is more powerful than you—in a sense—than I must find him. My only wish is to serve the most powerful man in the world. You are not that man."

And so without further ado, Reprobus left the King of Canaan and his castle, and set out to find the Devil.

And he did. Whenever you look for trouble, you are sure to find it. There behind a tree next to the road, he saw the Devil (though he did not know who he was at the time). Every time people would pass by, the Devil would jump out from behind the tree and scare them—they would run away as fast as their legs could carry them.

And when the Devil got tired of that, he would tell lies. Once a young man asked him, "Sir, which way is north? I am traveling to visit my mother and I have lost my way."

Then the Devil pointed south, but said, "That way is north." And the poor young man who trusted him walked the wrong way, and never got to see his mother.

Reprobus, who was new in the area, didn't know the difference between north and south. He didn't realize the Devil was lying.

Reprobus went to him and asked, "Where can I find the Devil, the most powerful man in the world?"

And the Devil answered, "I am the Devil. Follow me. I could use someone as big and strong as you. We'll stay on this road until we reach the next town."

So Reprobus followed the Devil down the road, but as they came near an old image of Christ on the Cross, the Devil started shaking, jumped off the road, and ran through a patch of briar, and made a wide circle around the image of Christ on the Cross.

Well, Reprobus followed the Devil through that patch of thistle and thorn bushes and got his legs all scratched up. Finally, when they got far enough away, the Devil once again took to the road.

You might be wondering why the Devil avoided passing the image of Christ on the Cross. Reprobus was wondering the same thing. He finally asked the Devil why he avoided passing that image along the road.

"I didn't avoid anything," said the Devil. "I just got tired of walking on the road."

Now Reprobus knew the Devil was lying because the Devil had looked so scared when he first noticed the old image. Reprobus also knew that nobody in his right mind would get his legs all scratched up walking through a field of thorn bushes when he could just as easily walk down a smooth road. So he turned and walked in the opposite direction.

"And where do you think you're going?" shouted the Devil.

"My only wish is to serve the most powerful man in the world. I am going to look for Christ, because he scared you."

Well, the Devil knew he could no longer argue that point, so he said, "Go. I hope you never find him."

Now the Devil's wish almost came true. Reprobus searched and searched, but could not find Christ.

He asked many people if they knew where he could find him. Some said, "I never heard of him." Others said, "In heaven, but you can't get there."

But one day, someone said, "I don't know, but I think I know of someone who could help you. An old hermit lives in a cave near the hill in the middle of the desert. Ask him."

So Reprobus walked all day hoping to find the middle of the desert where the old hermit lived. It was very hot and he was getting very thirsty. He walked and walked. The sun made him dizzy. At times, he didn't think he would make it. Finally he saw the hill and caves in the distance. Although he was very hot and thirsty and tired, he ran until he came to the hill where he found the cave the old hermit lived in.

As he went into the old hermit's cave, he saw the hermit was stirring a little pot over the fire cooking some rice and beans.

"Old Hermit," said Reprobus, "tell me where I can find Christ."

"Sit down," said the hermit. "Here, you look thirsty. Drink some water from this jug."

"No," said Reprobus, "First tell me where I can find Christ."

"No," said the hermit. "First drink the water, and have something to eat. Then I will tell you how to find Christ."

Reprobus did as he was told. He drank the entire jug of water, and then he ate all the rice and beans the hermit gave him. Then the hermit led Reprobus outside where they both sat down and leaned against the wall of the cave. Reprobus knew he had to be patient.

It grew dark. They just sat and watched all the stars come out. Later, Reprobus and the hermit saw the full moon.

Finally the hermit said, "Well, if you want to find Christ, you must fast, that is, not eat or drink anything for a long time."

"I can't do that," said Reprobus. "I will grow sick and weak. I can't do that."

"Well," said that hermit, "then you must pray."

"I don't know how to pray," said Reprobus. "I can't do that either."

The old hermit thought and thought. "I know," he said. "I know exactly what is best for you. North of here, as you leave the desert, you will see mountains. Just before you get there, you will find a forest with a road running through it. In the middle of the forest is a dangerous river. Many people who try to cross it are carried downstream and are never seen or heard of again. Go to that river. You are big and strong. Help people cross it. Carry them over to the other side. You sure look strong enough."

"But I want to find Christ, the most powerful man in the world. I want to serve him," said Reprobus.

The old hermit looked into his face and said, "Reprobus, I know what I'm talking about. I think you will meet Christ there."

"But how will I know him? What does he look like?" asked Reprobus.

But all the hermit would say is, "Go to the river. Help other people cross over. I think you will meet Christ there."

As you may suspect, Reprobus left the hermit, traveled north to the edge of the desert, saw the mountains, and found the road leading through the forest, and finally, the raging river.

It was peaceful and green there in the middle of the trees. Reprobus liked to listen to the sound of the river. He decided to build a house there and spent many years carrying people across the river.

He really began to like helping people. It made him feel good when they thanked him for carrying them across. And they didn't run away when he asked them if he could help them. This made him happy too.

Some people would try to cross the river alone. Soon after, he would hear them hollering for help. Then he would run into the river, help them onto his back, and carry them to the other side. Once on the other side, they would cry and say, "Thank you for saving my life."

One night, it grew very dark and windy and cold. Reprobus knew a storm was coming up. He went inside and made a fire. It was warm and quiet inside, but he could hear the wind howling, and the branches of the trees scratching against his house, and the rain thumping on his roof. Then he heard something strange—it was a child's voice, and it was saying, "Please help me."

He got up, opened the door, looked outside, but he could see no one. He just felt the rain and heard the rush of the river.

He went back in, closed the door, but then he heard the voice again, "Reprobus, help me."

Again he opened the door, walked outside, but could see no one. He went back inside, but just before he could close the door, again he heard, "Help me. Please help me."

This time he walked out of his house and down to the bank of the river. With his hand he shielded his eyes from the rain, and there, on the other side, to his surprise, stood a little child holding a ball in his hand. "Please carry me across," the child cried.

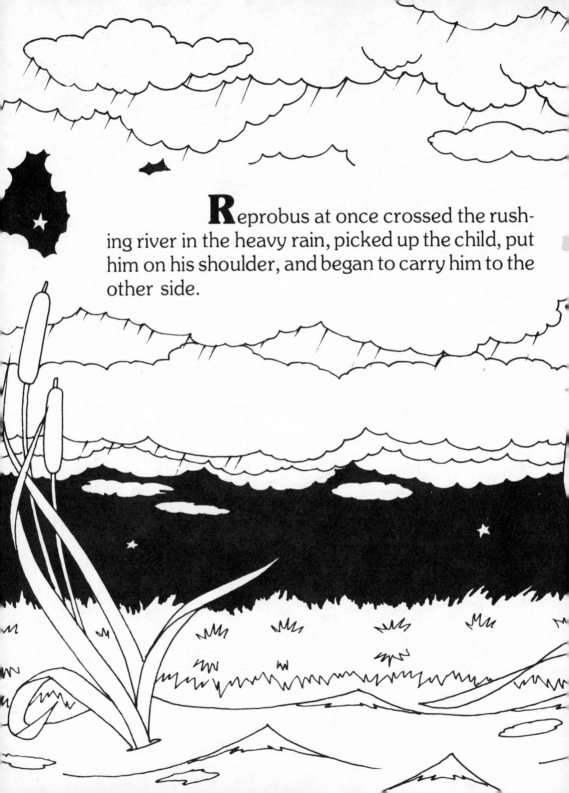

Reprobus at once crossed the rushing river in the heavy rain, picked up the child, put him on his shoulder, and began to carry him to the other side.

He was wondering what a little child was doing out alone on a night like this, when he felt the little boy get heavier, and heavier, and heavier—so heavy, in fact, that he didn't think he'd make it to the other side. He started to fall, but just then a big pole floated by. He grabbed it and stuck it in the river till it hit bottom, to steady himself. Then he used it as a cane to help himself carry the child to the other side.

Somehow he climbed up the bank and bent down to let the child climb down from his shoulder; then he had to sit down to catch his breath.

Finally he said, "Little boy, you got so heavy, I thought I was carrying the world on my shoulder."

"You were," said the little boy, "and you were also carrying the one who made the world. I am Christ the King, the one you have been looking for, the one you wish to serve. Whenever you carry anyone across the river, you are helping me—and the world becomes lighter for me to carry." And with that, the little ball he held in his hand began to glow—and Reprobus understood the little ball to be the world.

Then the Christ Child vanished—and Reprobus was alone again in the rain.

As his strength came back, he got up with the help of the pole, and walked back to his house. He stuck the pole in the wet earth outside the door, went inside, fell on his bed, and fell fast asleep.

The next morning, the sun was shining through his window and woke him from sleep. He slowly got out of bed, opened the door, and walked outside.

There to his surprise, he saw that the pole he had stuck in the earth the night before had broken into bloom. It was a flowering tree—a gift from the Christ Child whom he had carried.

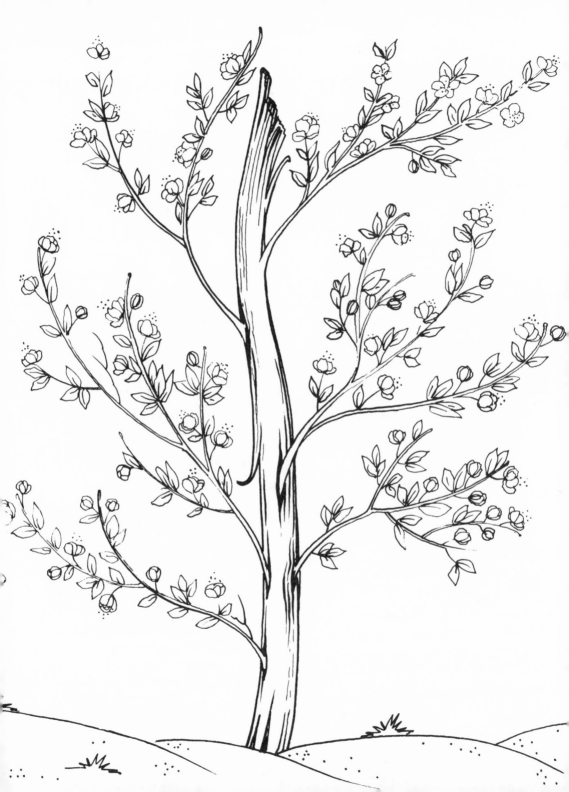

And that is the legend of Saint Christopher whose name used to be Reprobus. The new name he chose was Christopher which means "the Christ Carrier" or "the one who carries Christ."

People pray to Saint Christopher for help and protection while they travel.

And now do you know why Christopher is the only one of the saints shown carrying the Christ Child on his shoulder?

Pages for Drawing

Pages for Drawing

Pages for Drawing

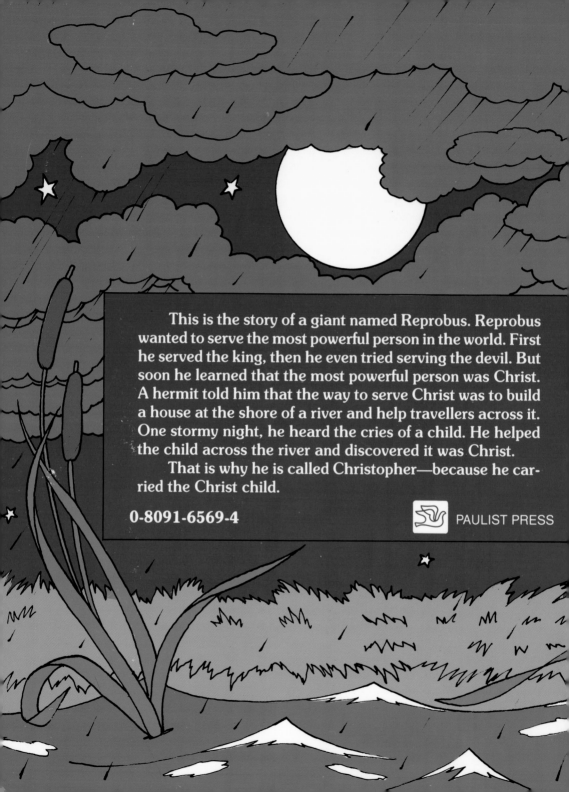

This is the story of a giant named Reprobus. Reprobus wanted to serve the most powerful person in the world. First he served the king, then he even tried serving the devil. But soon he learned that the most powerful person was Christ. A hermit told him that the way to serve Christ was to build a house at the shore of a river and help travellers across it. One stormy night, he heard the cries of a child. He helped the child across the river and discovered it was Christ.

That is why he is called Christopher—because he carried the Christ child.

0-8091-6569-4

PAULIST PRESS